Frog Coloring Book For Adults

This Coloring book belongs to:

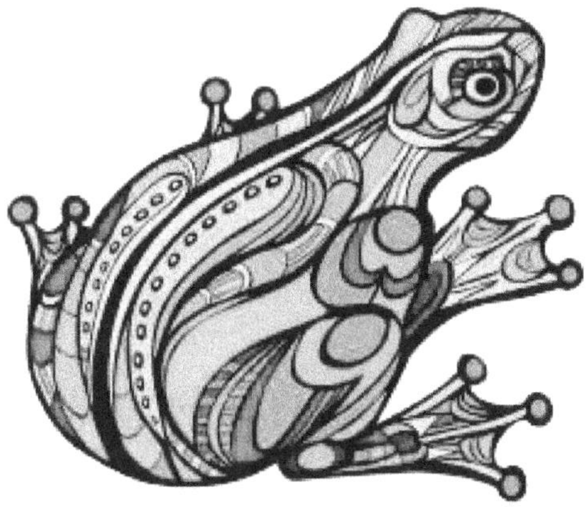

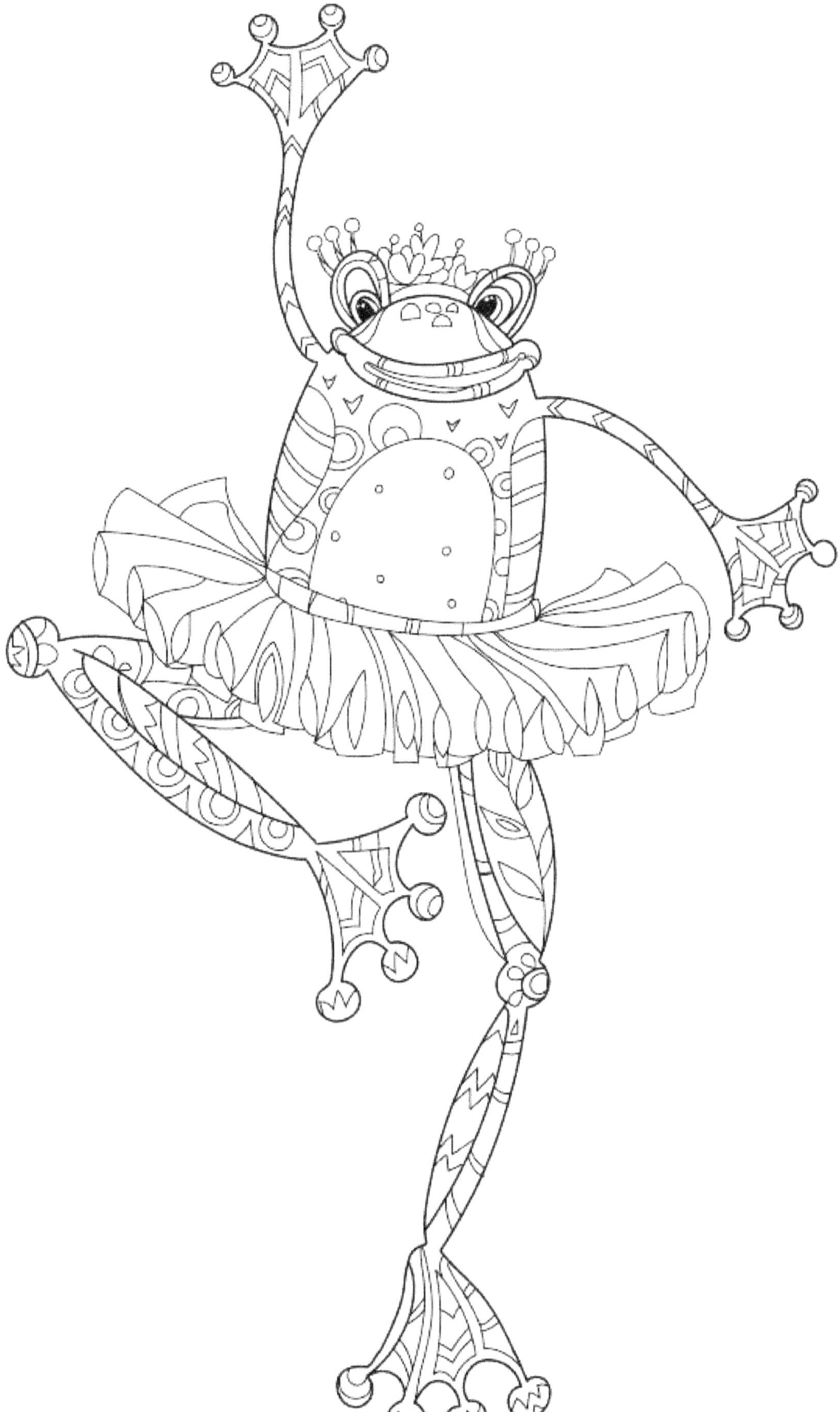

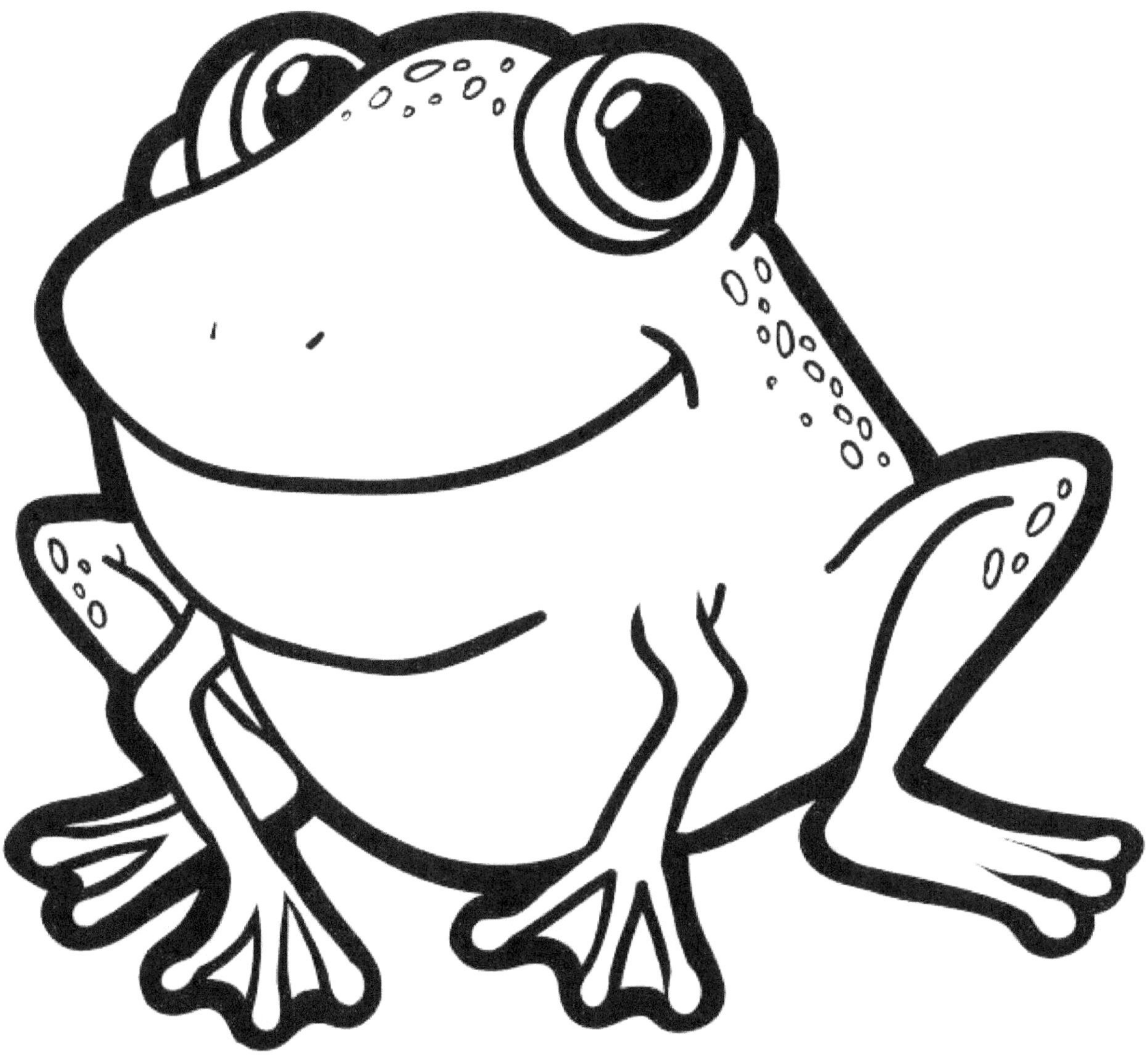

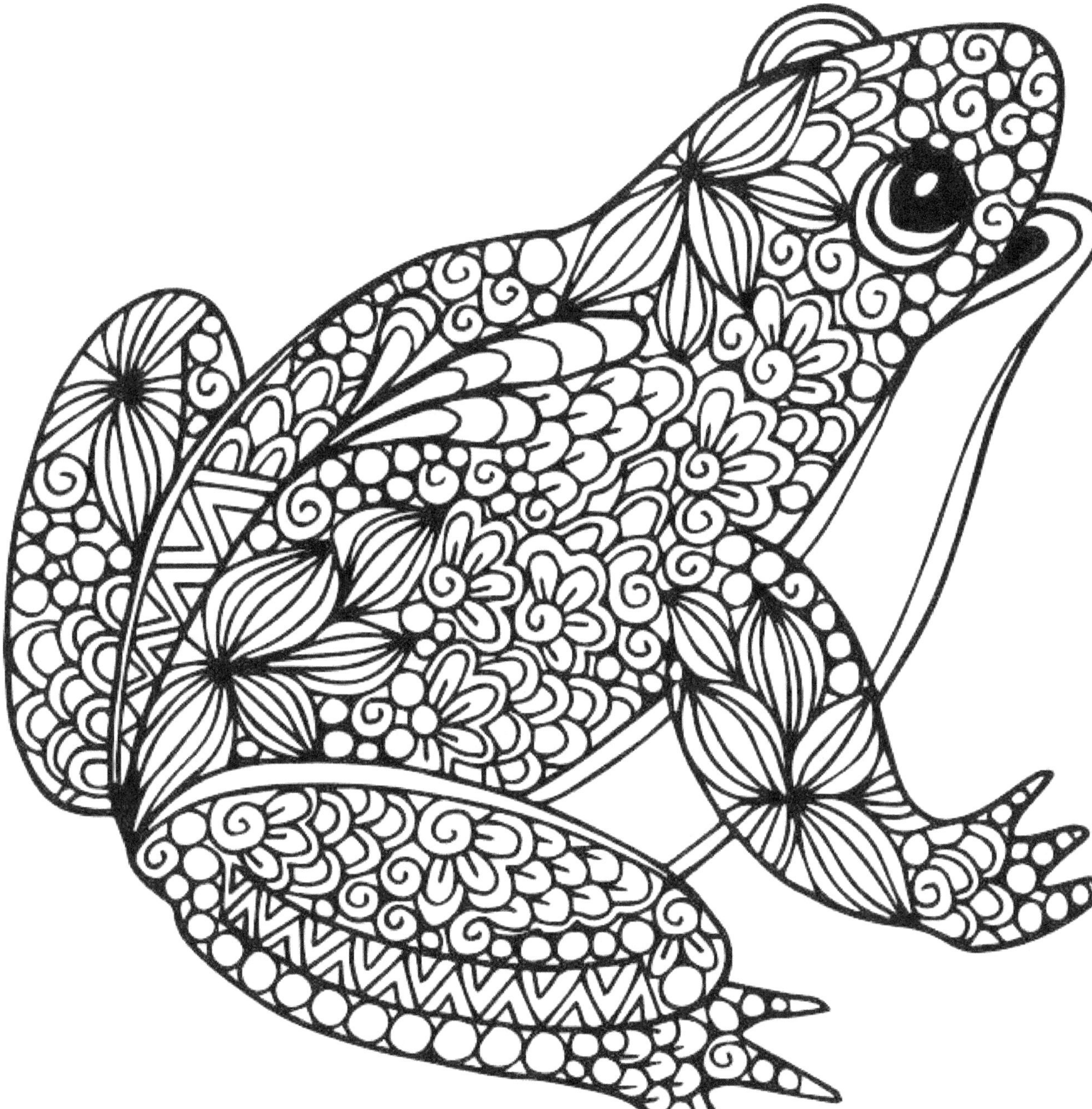

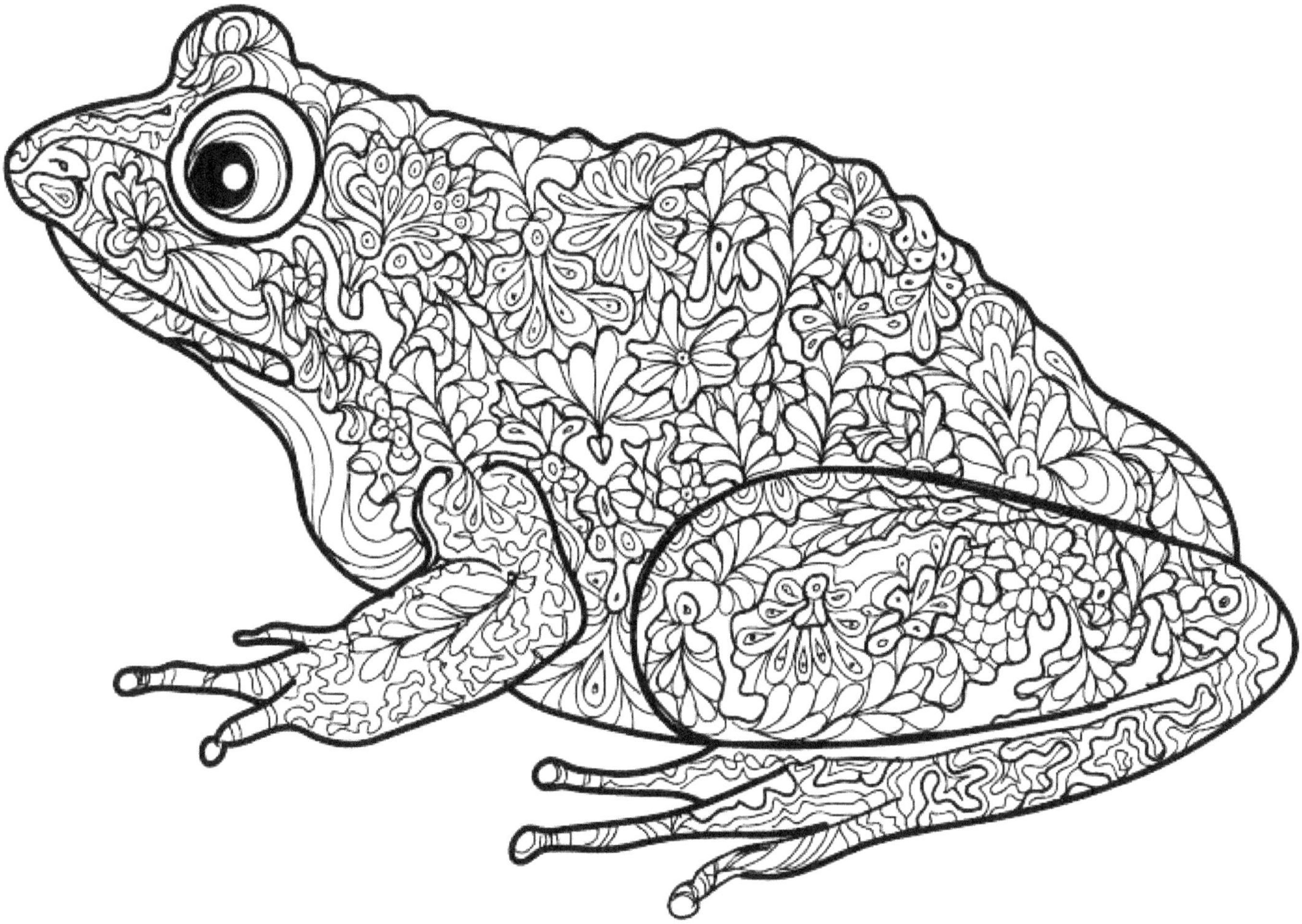

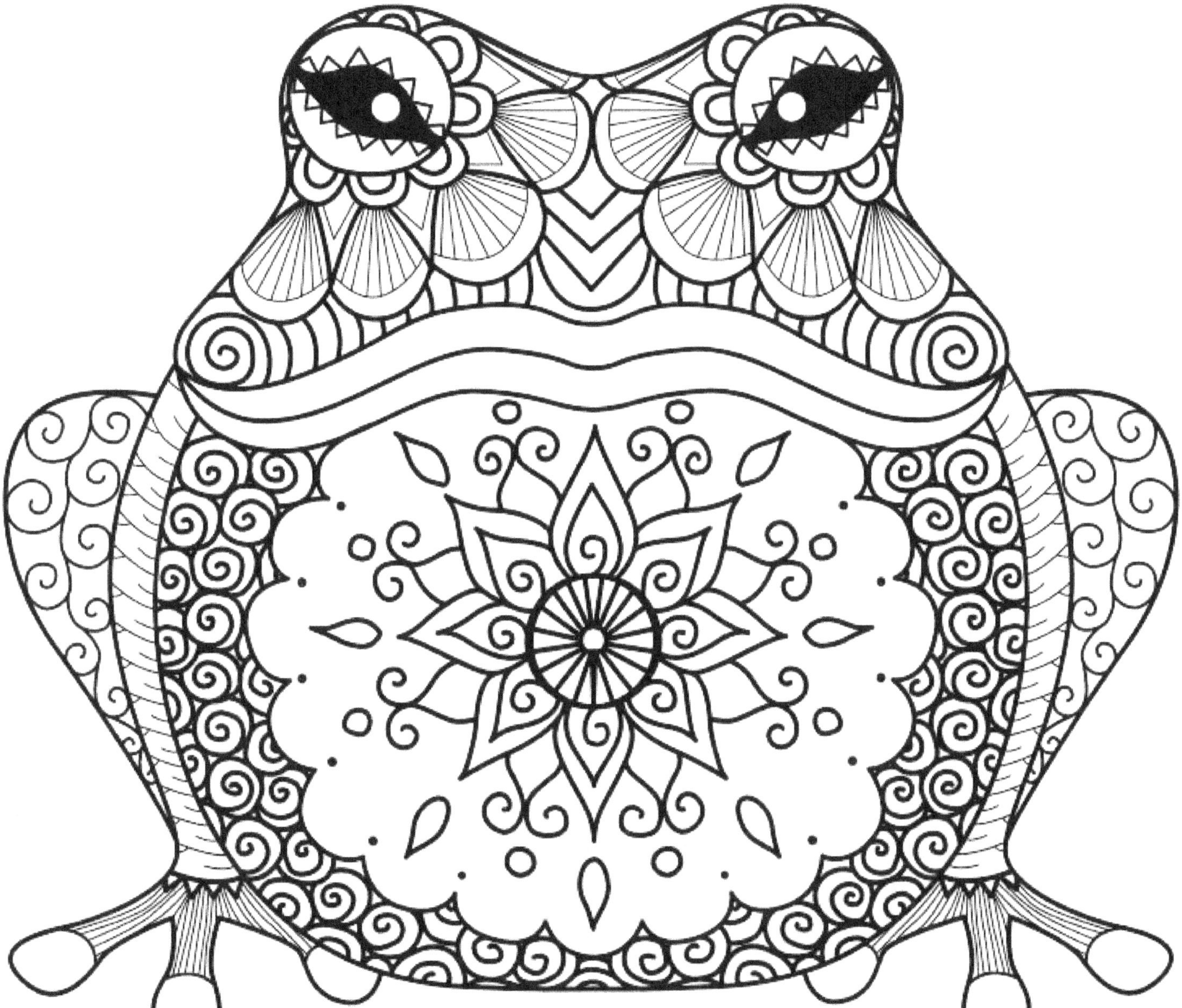

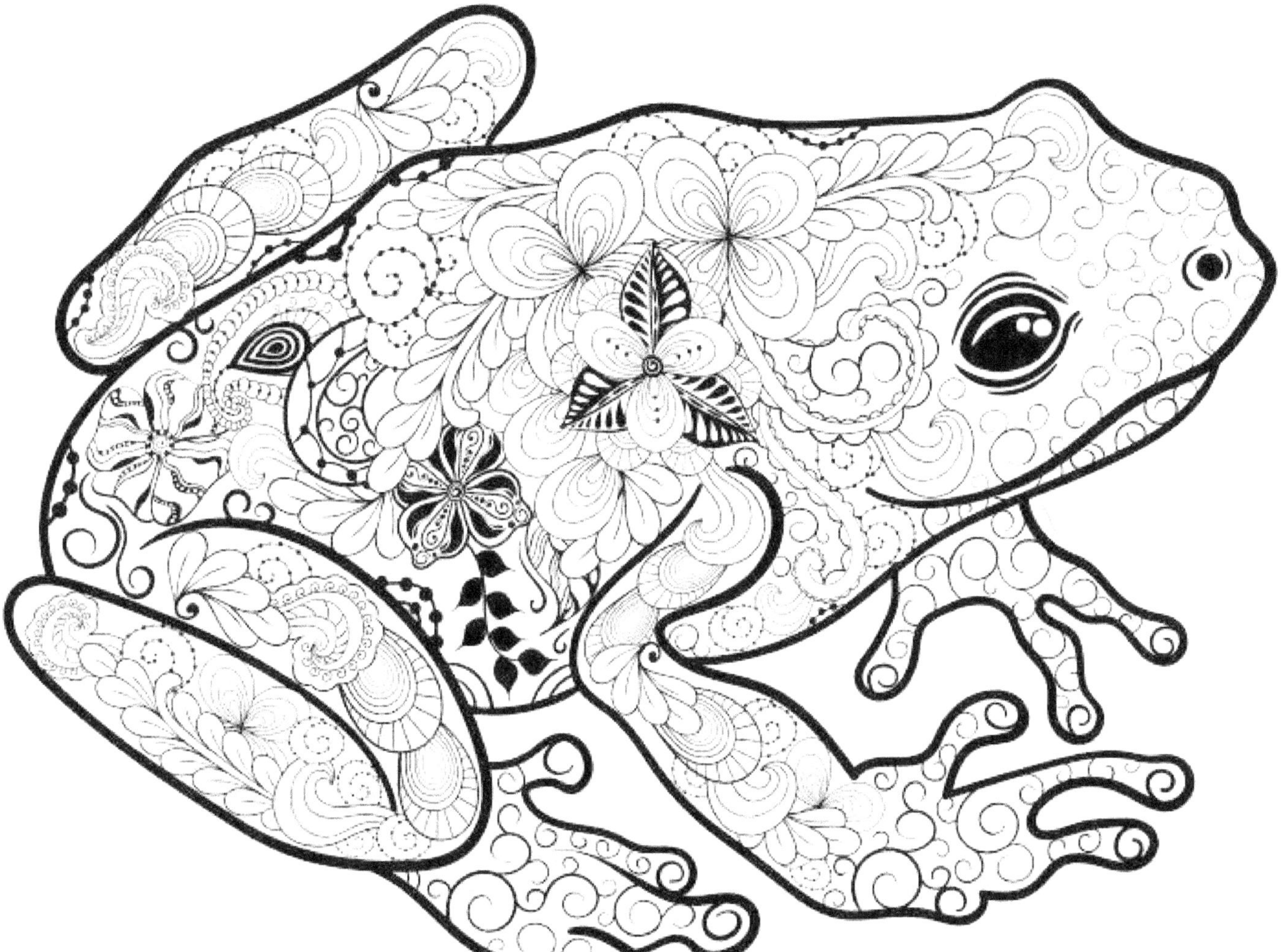

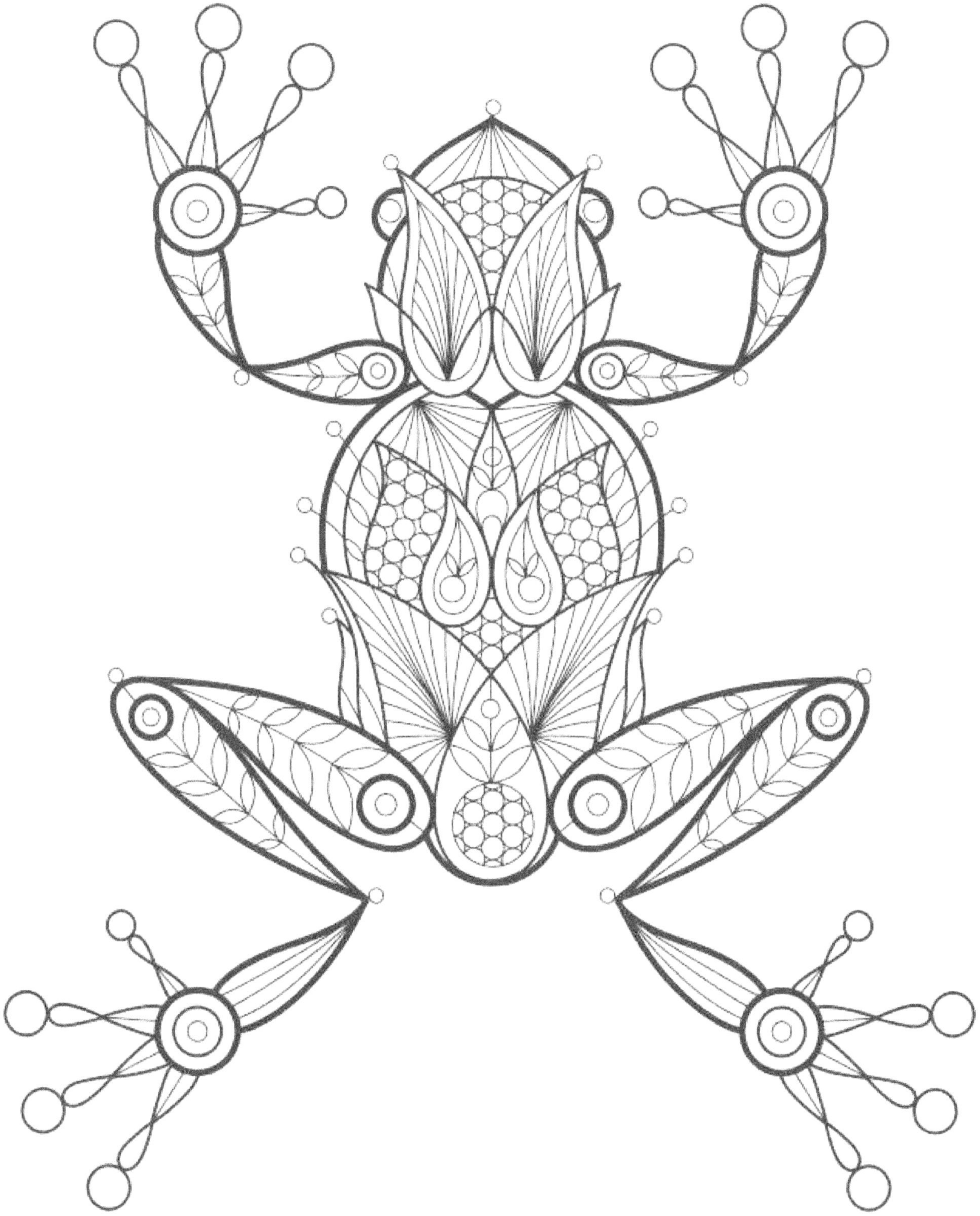

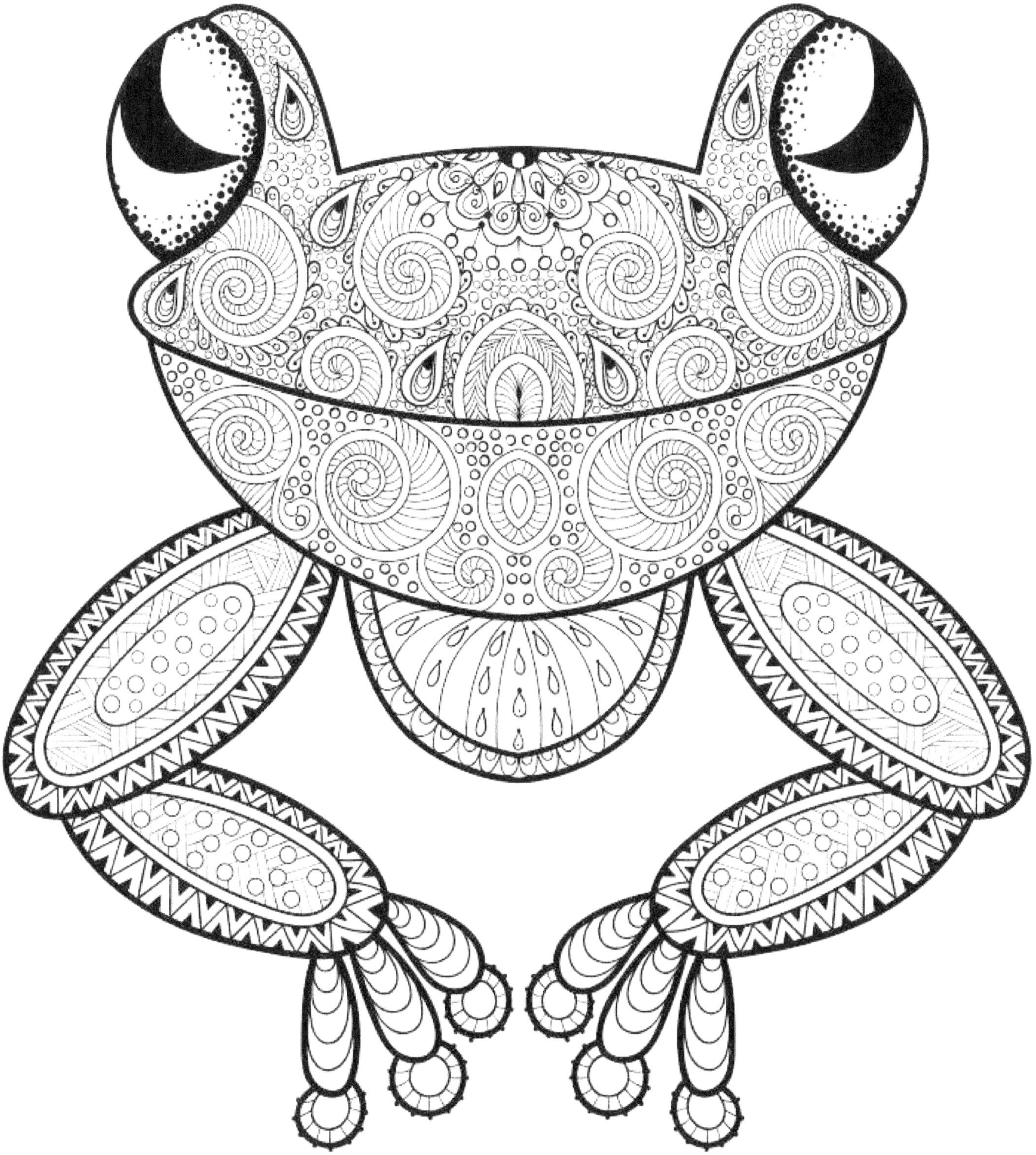

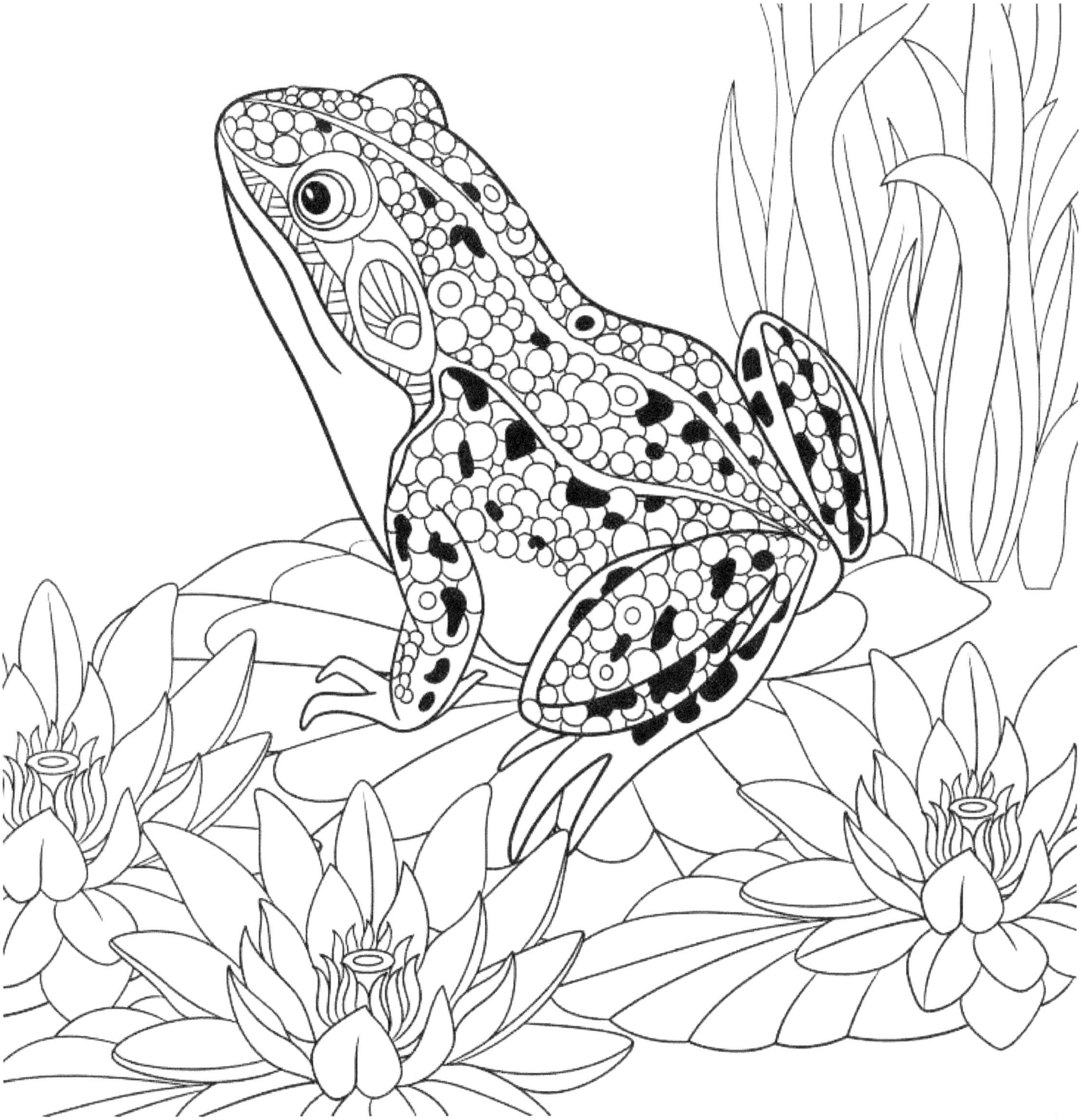

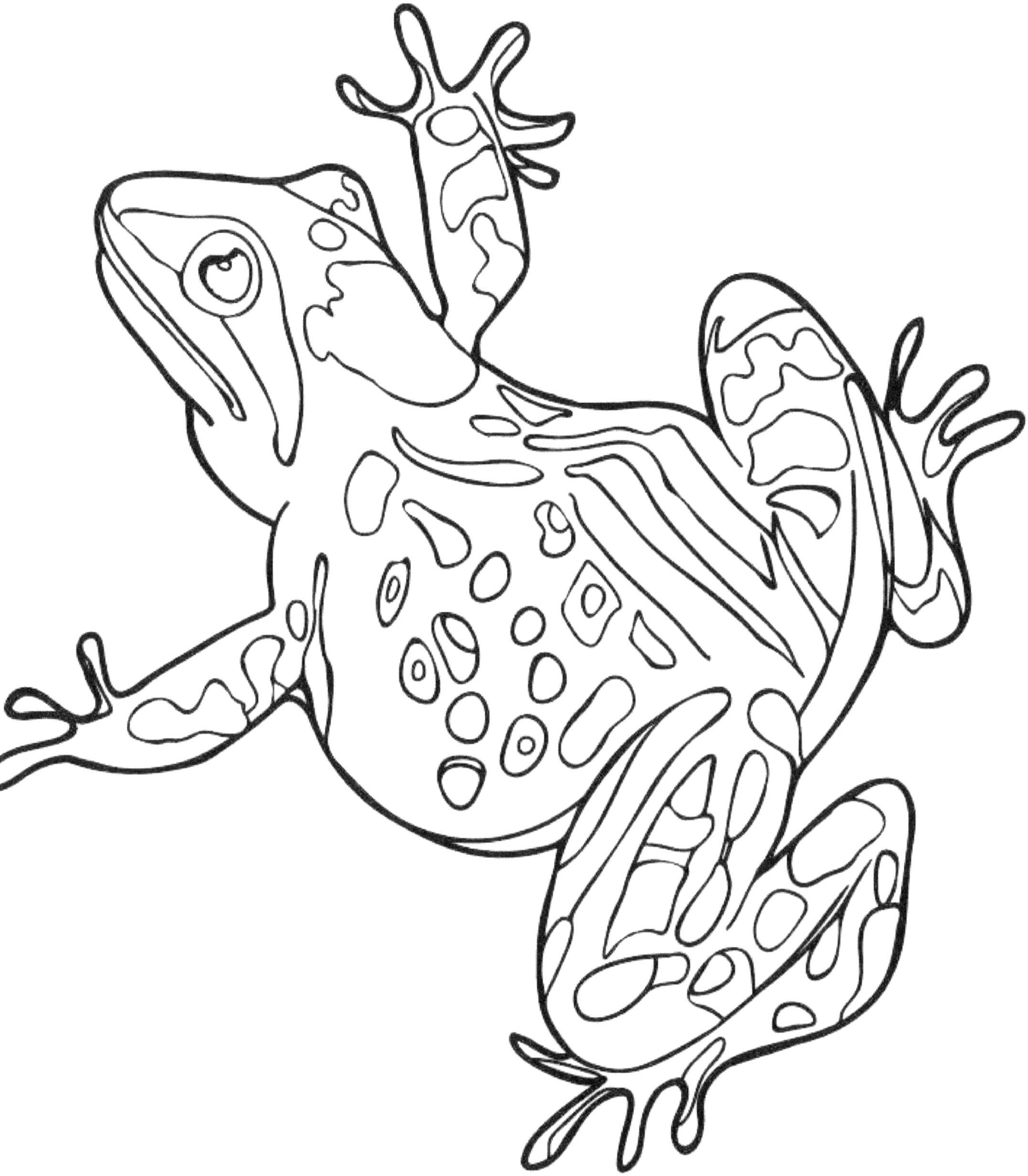

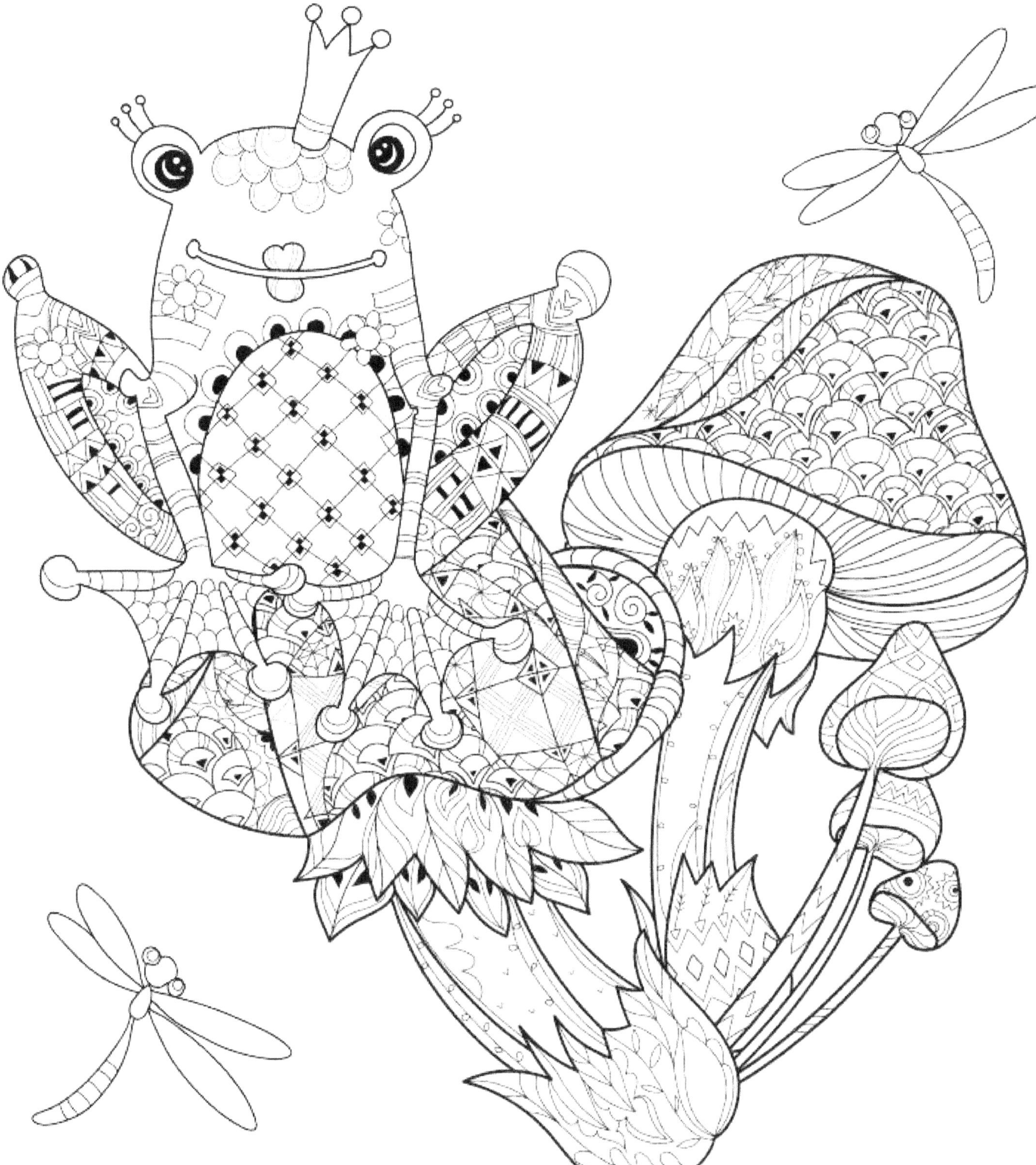

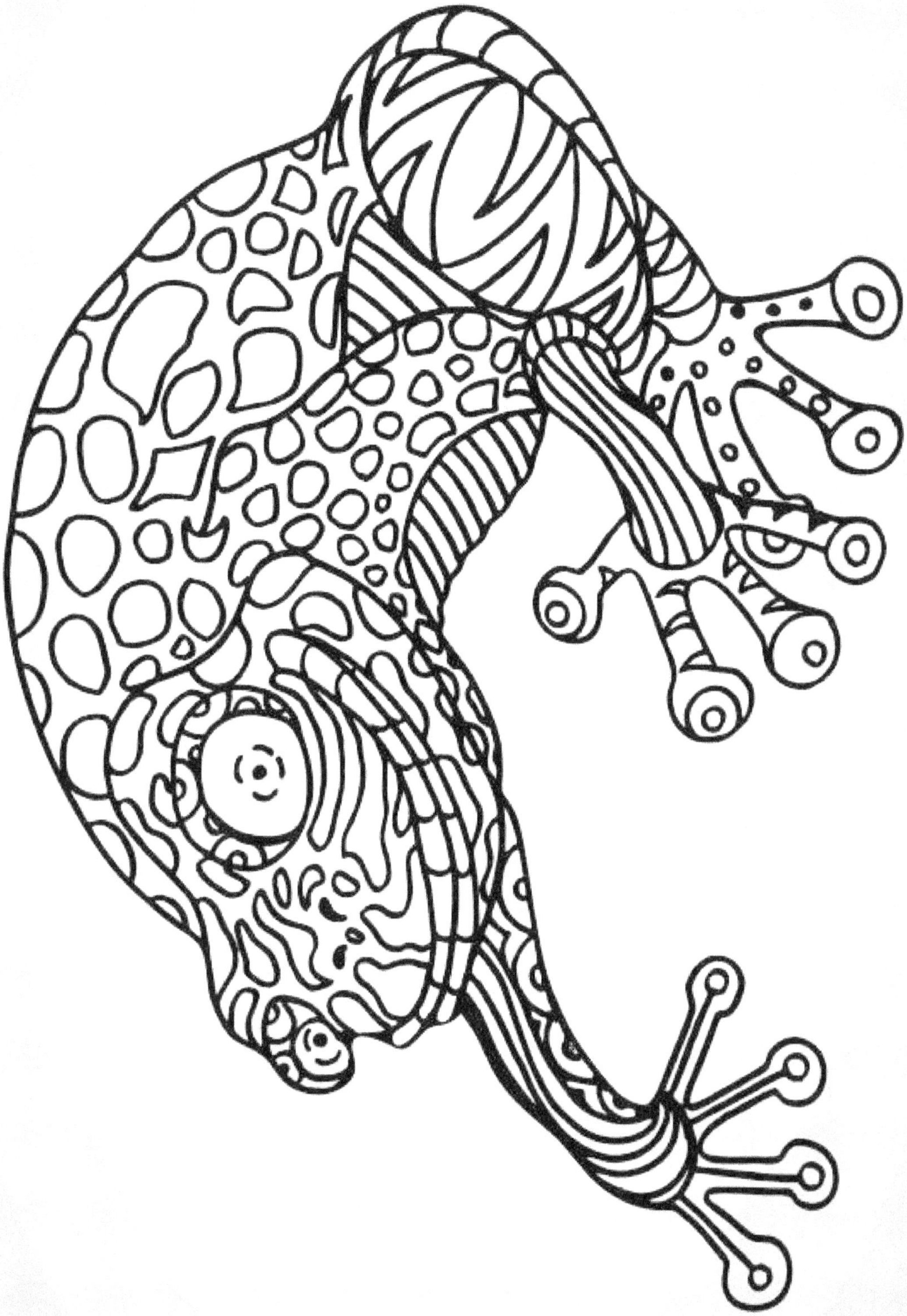

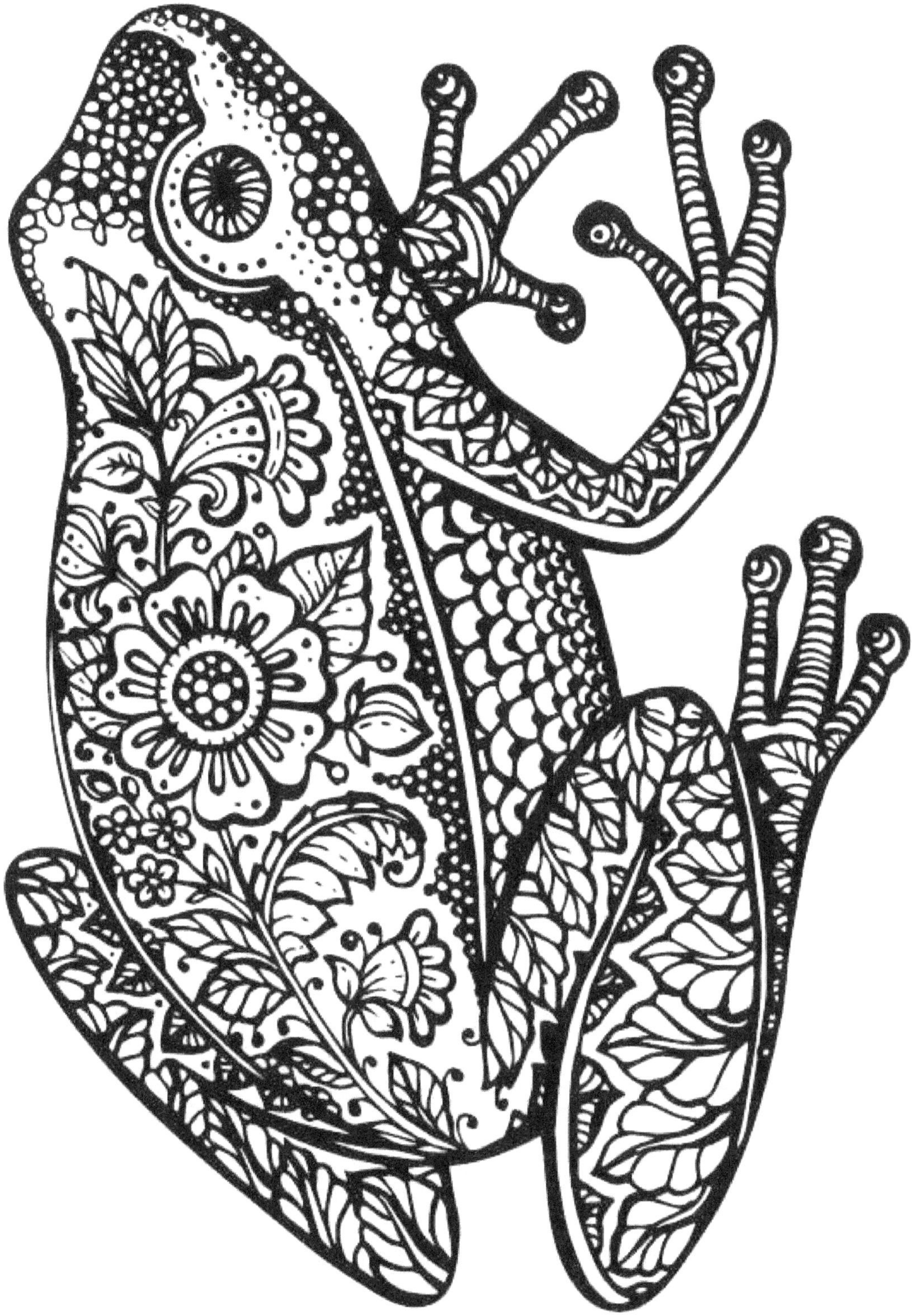

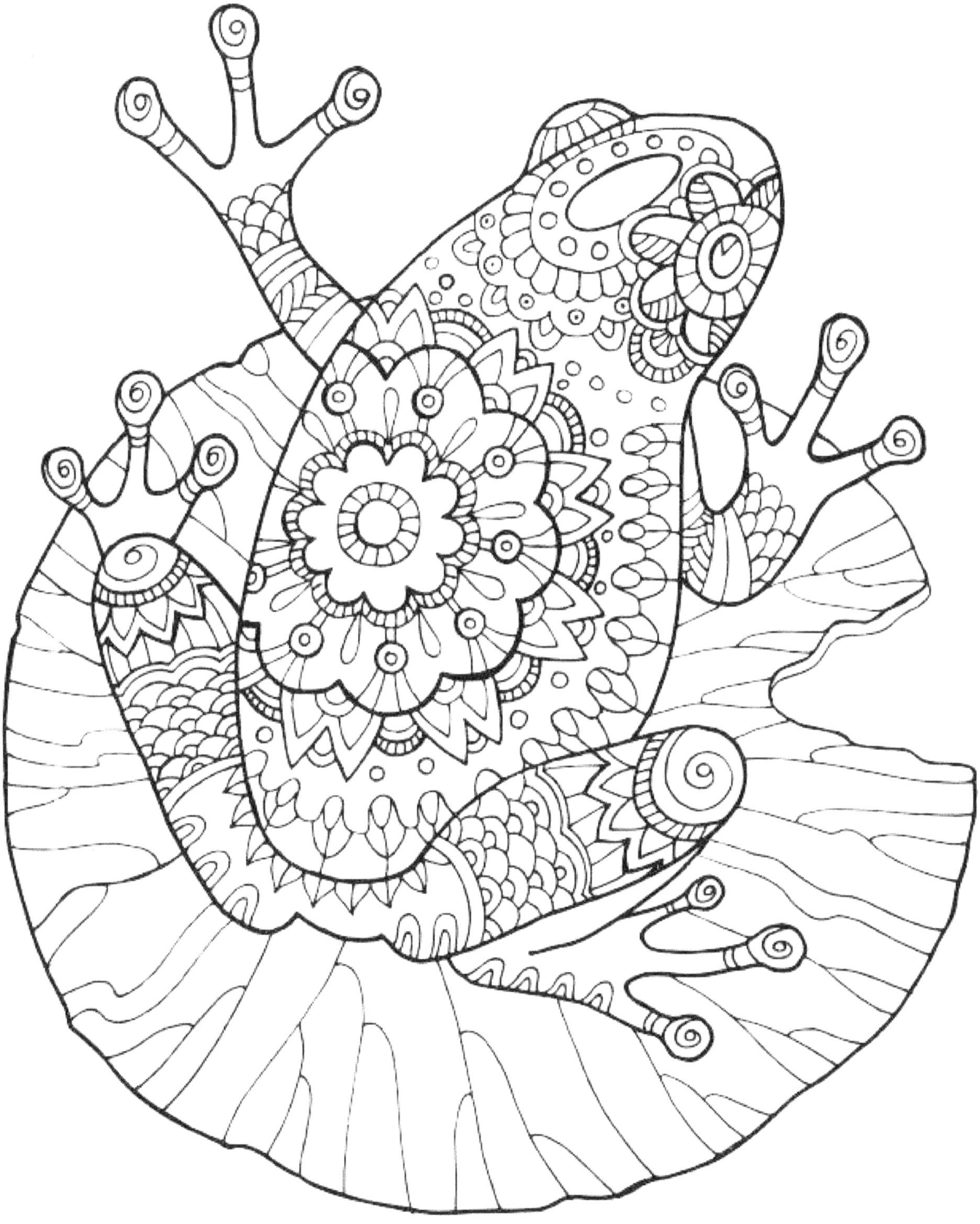

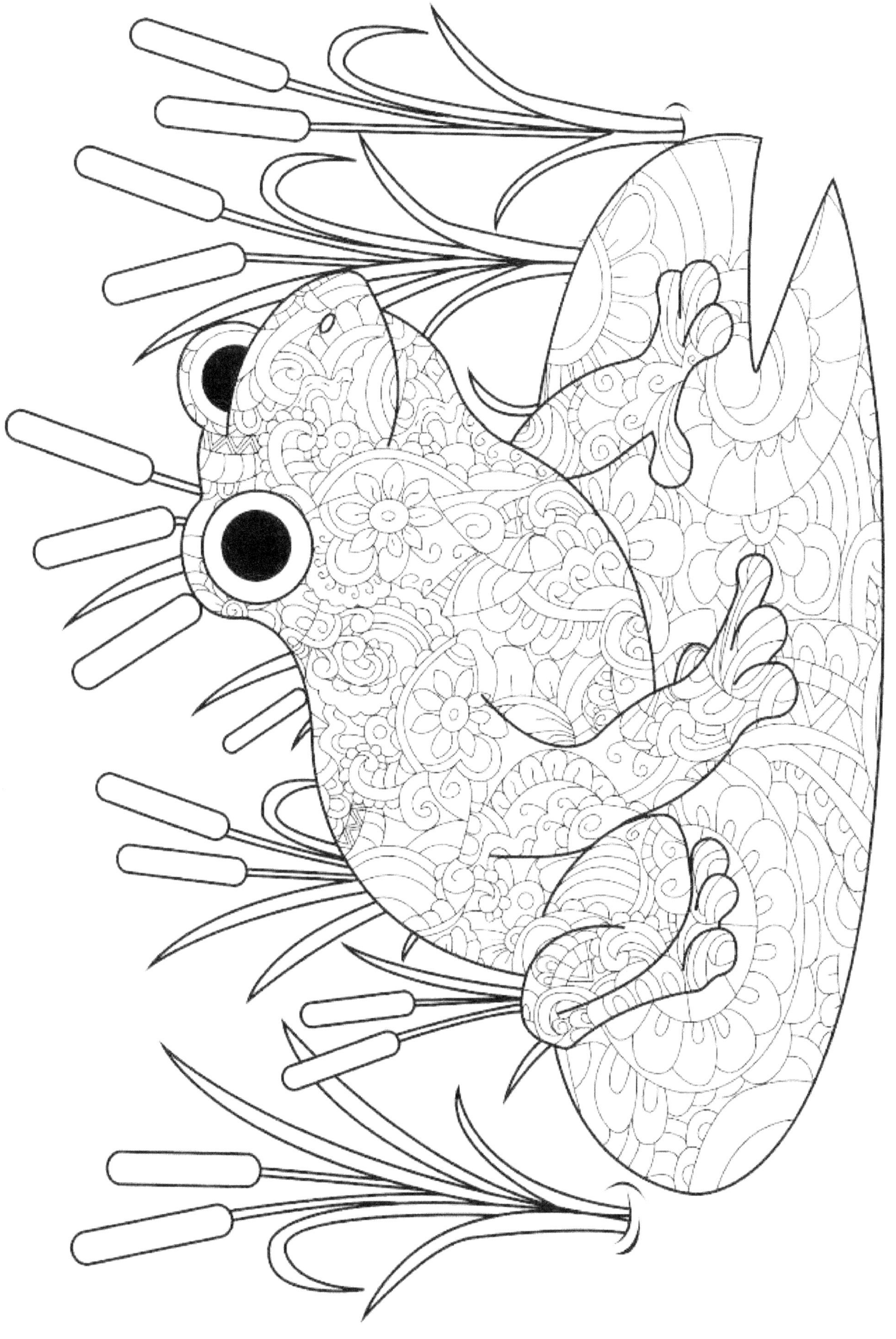

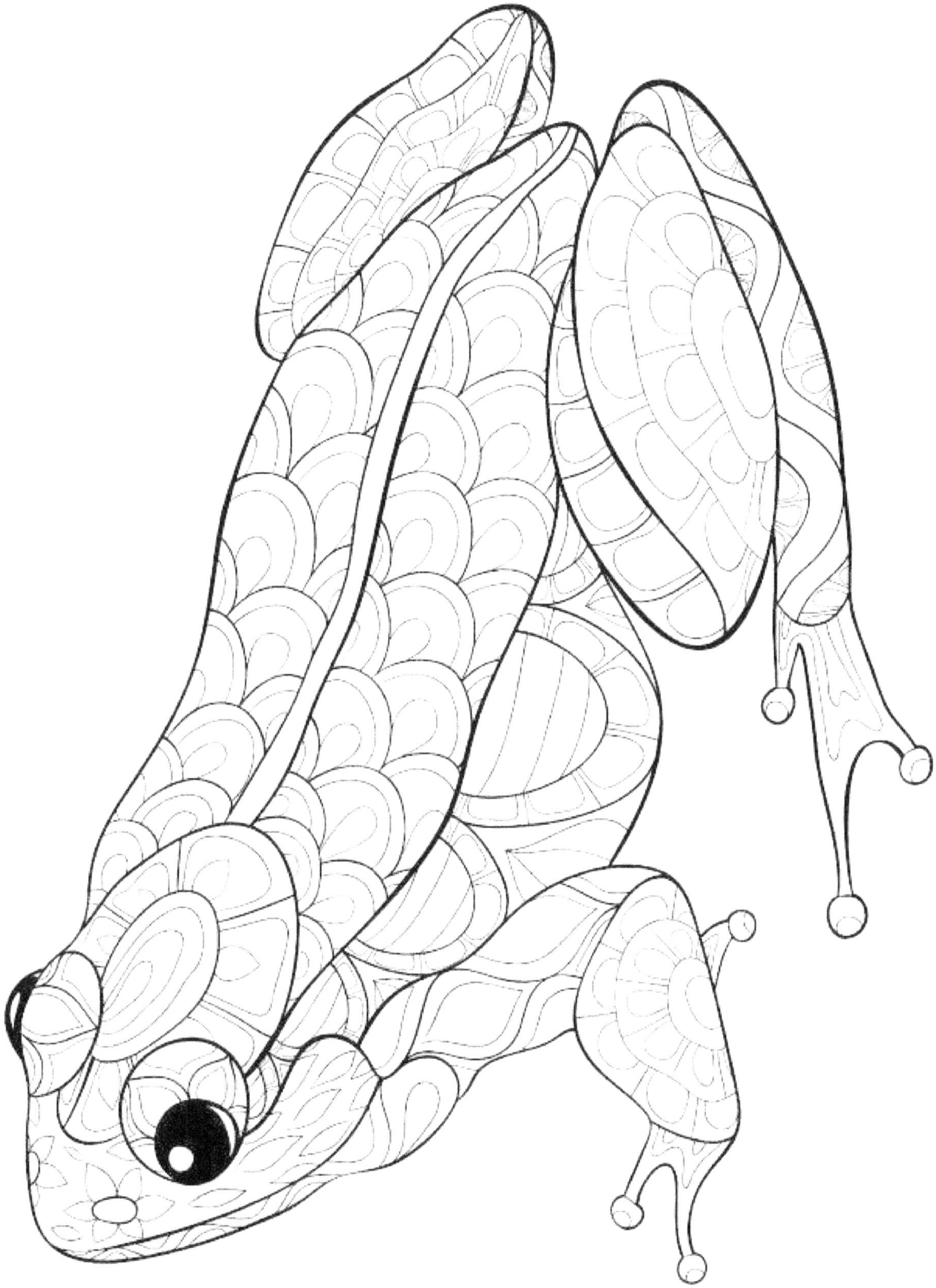

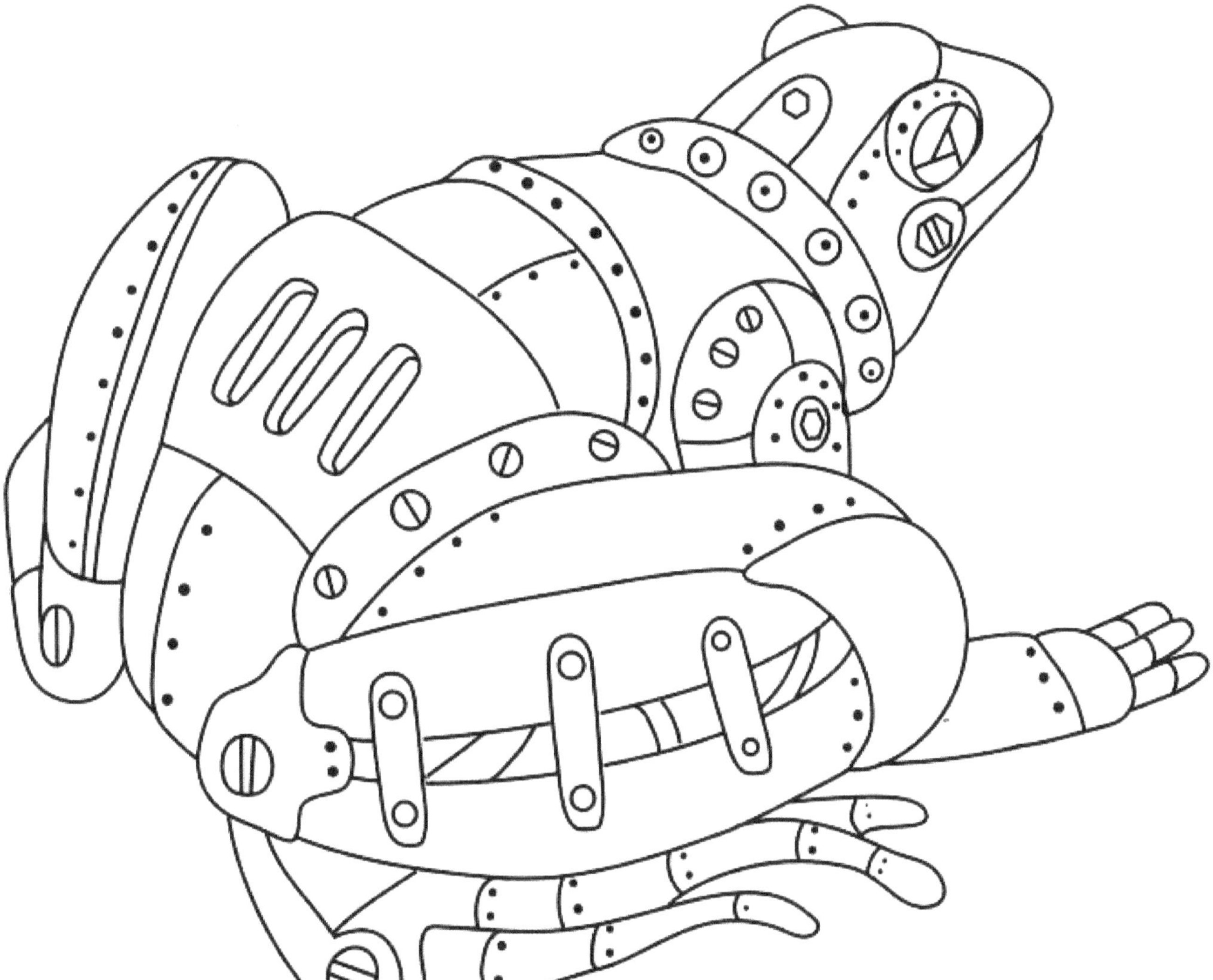

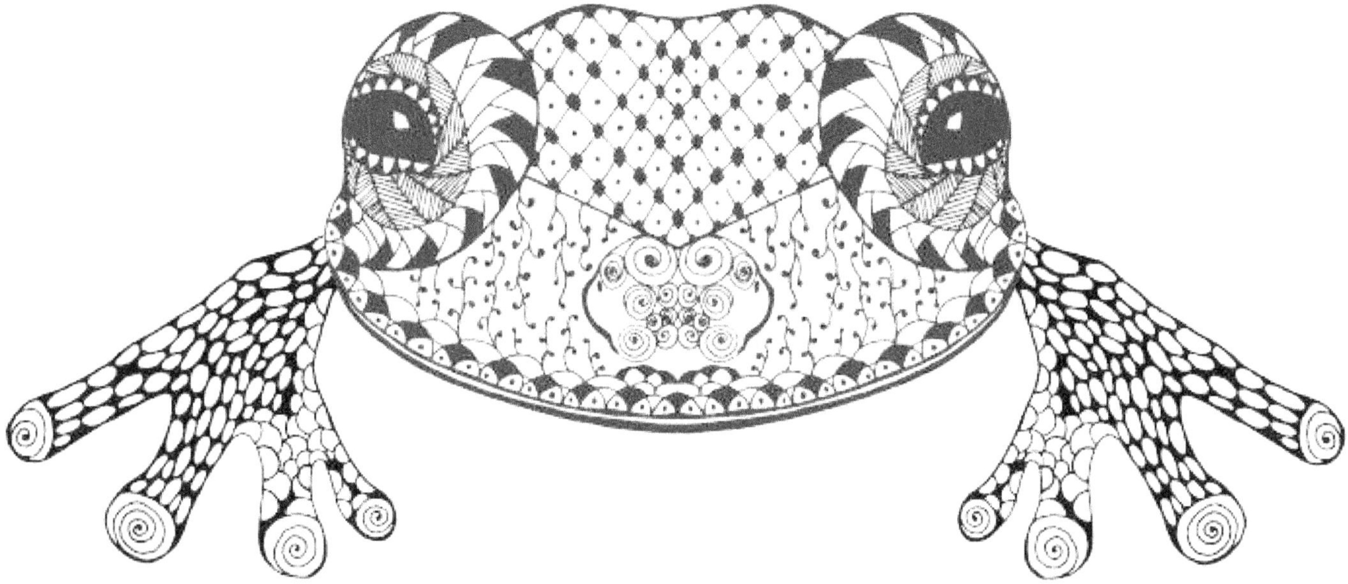

Surprise Bonus Sea Turtles Coloring Pages!

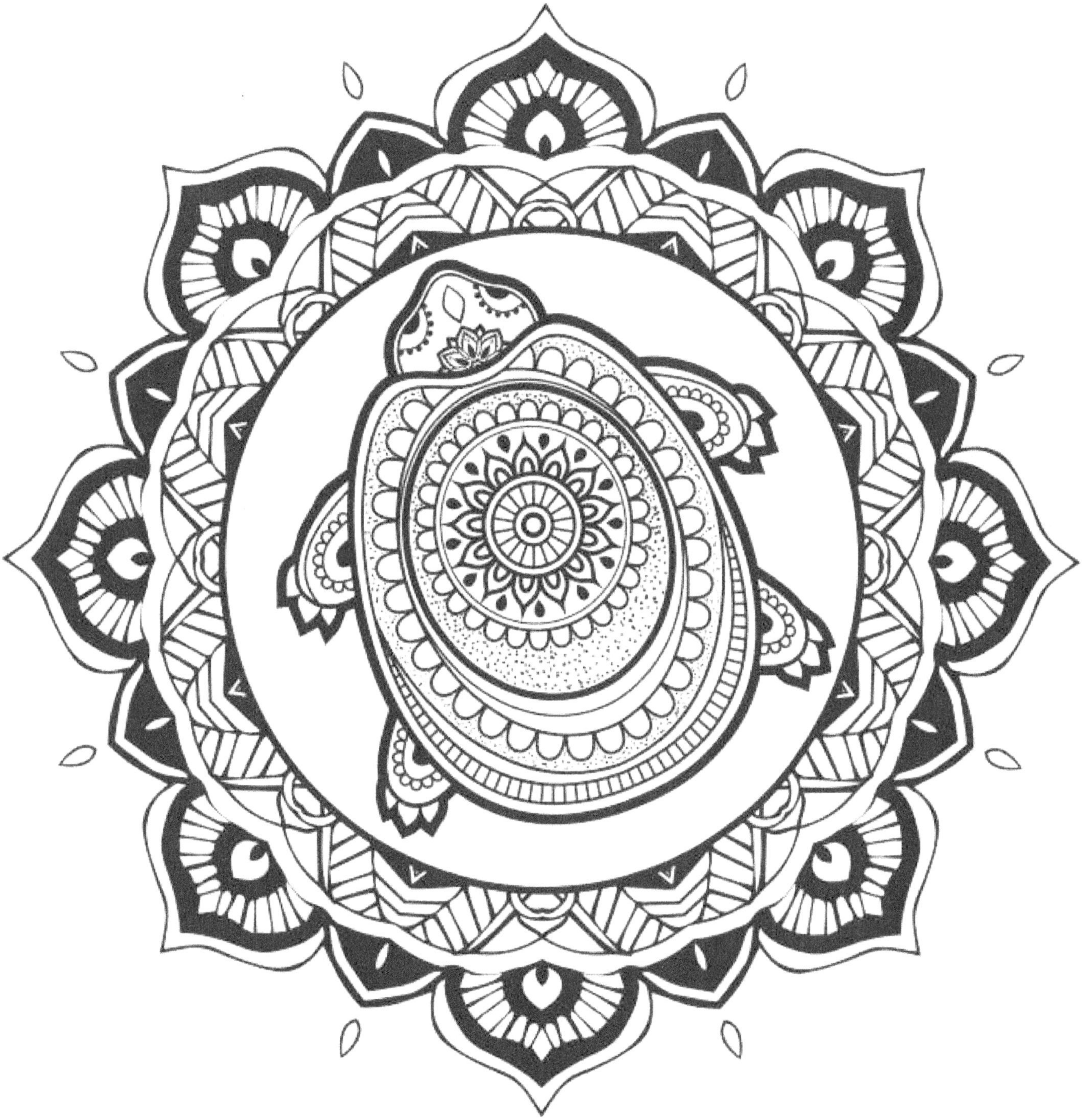

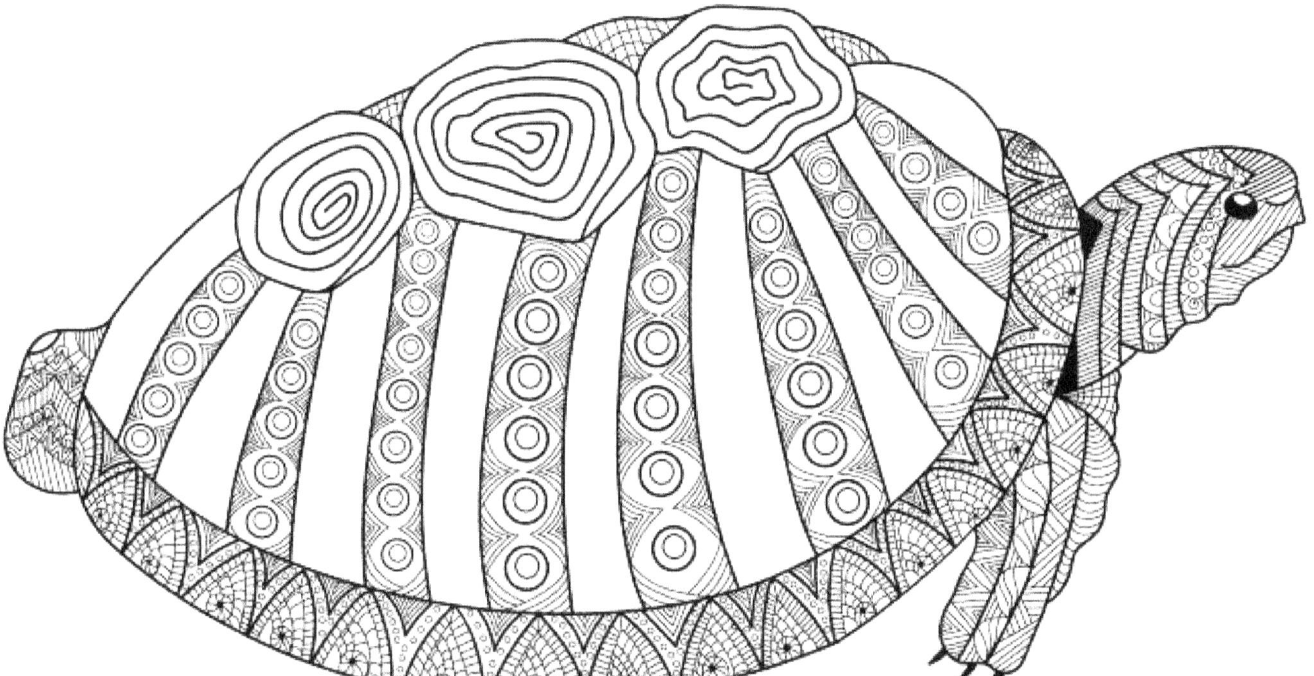

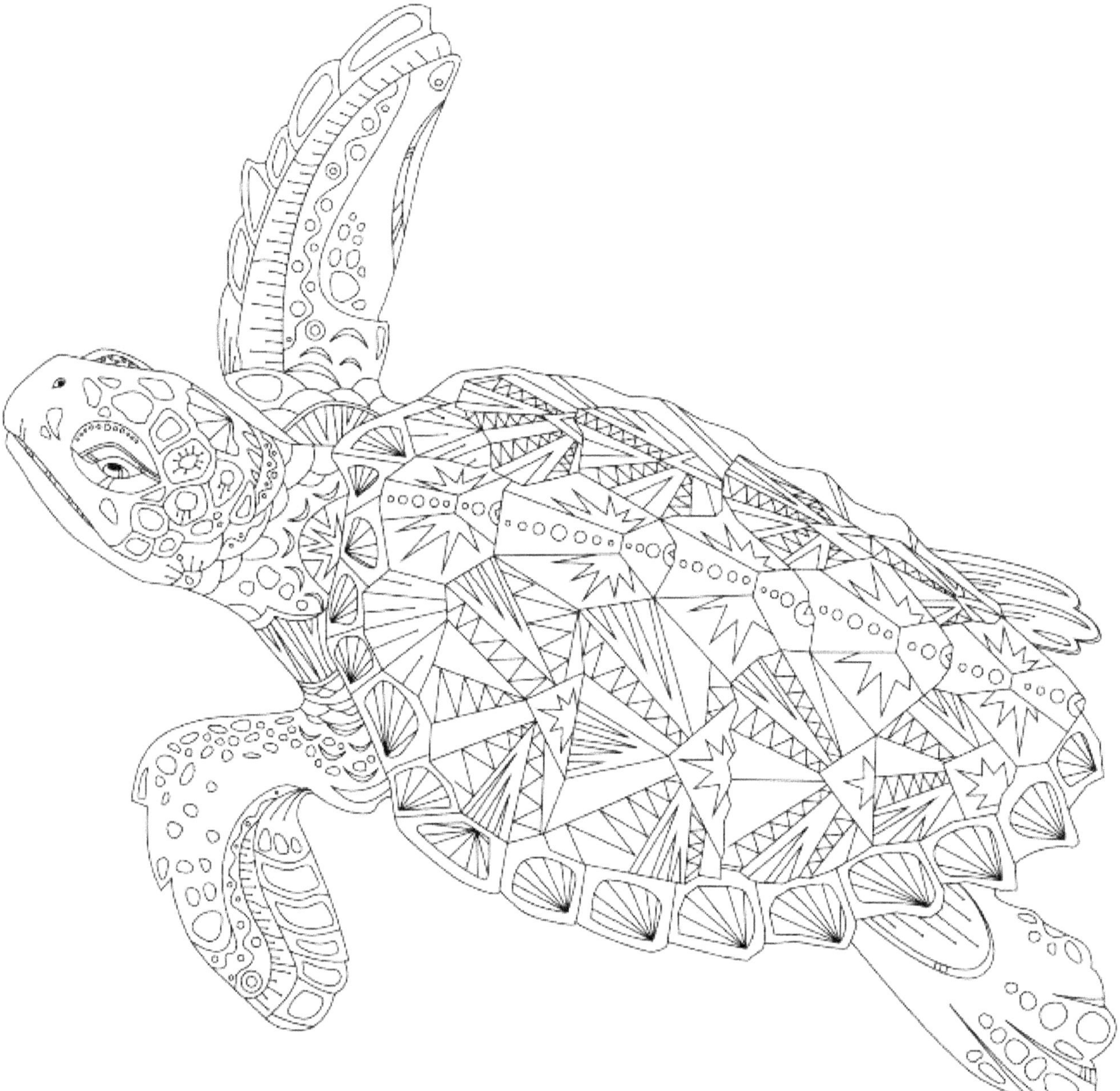

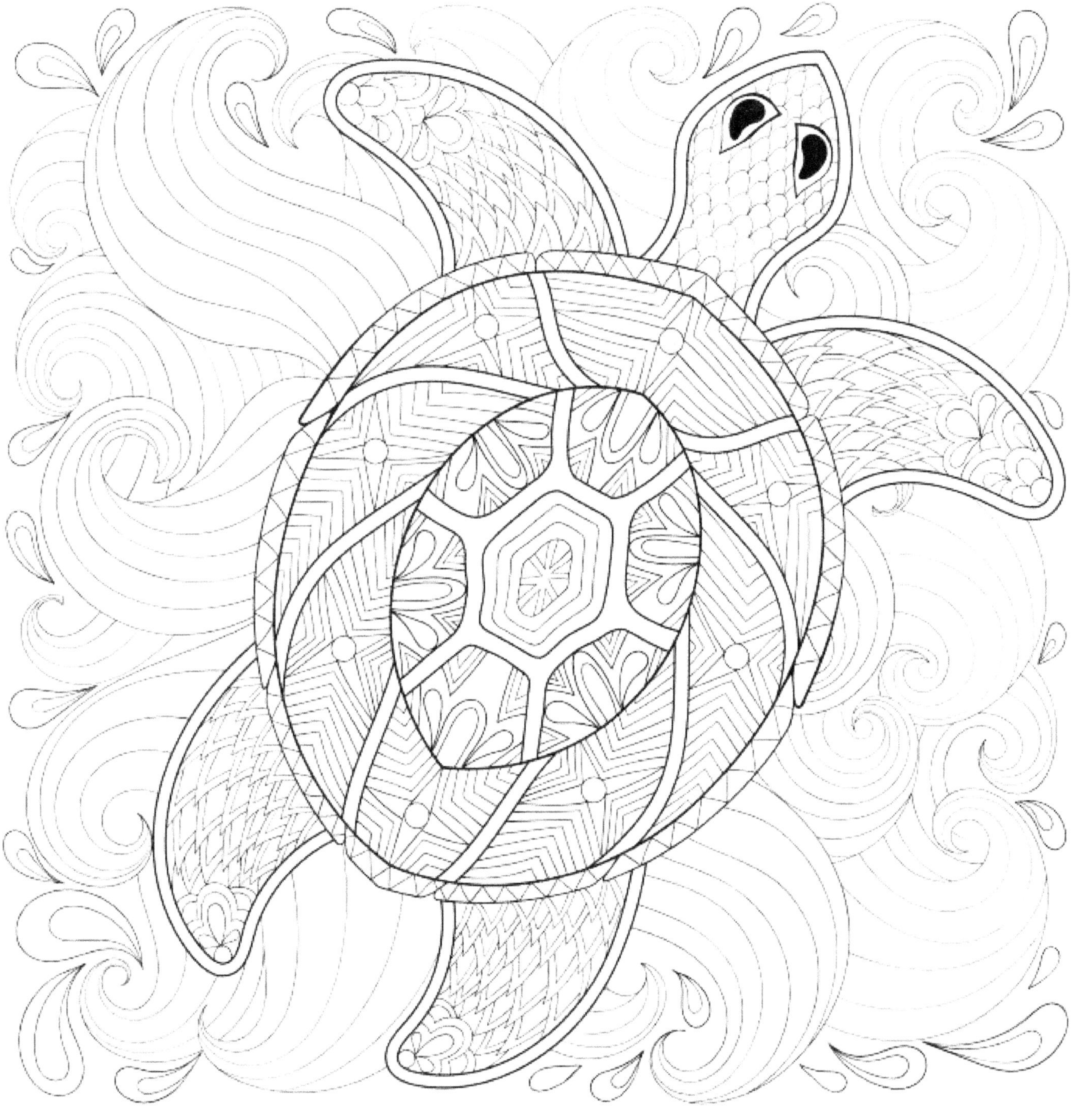

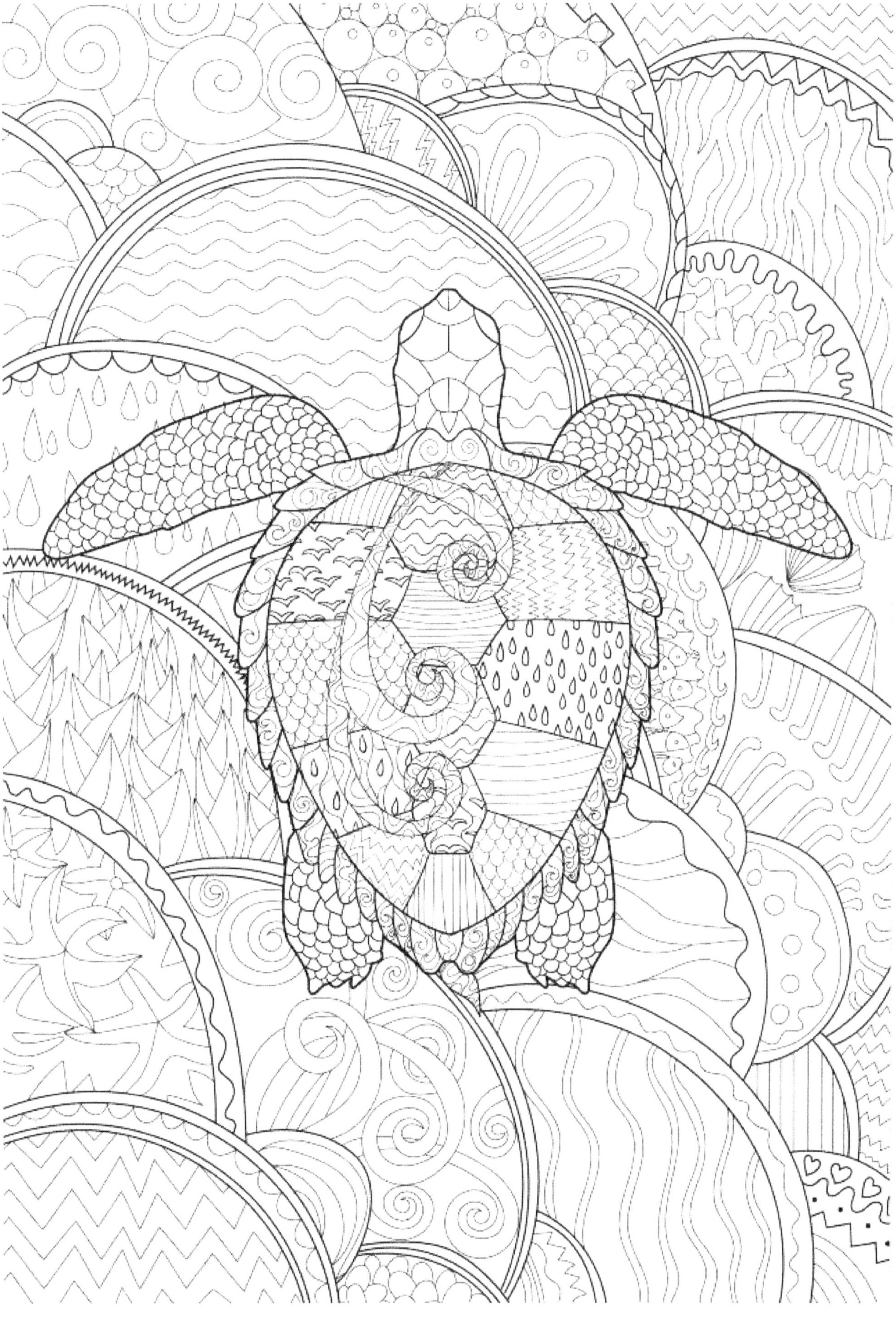

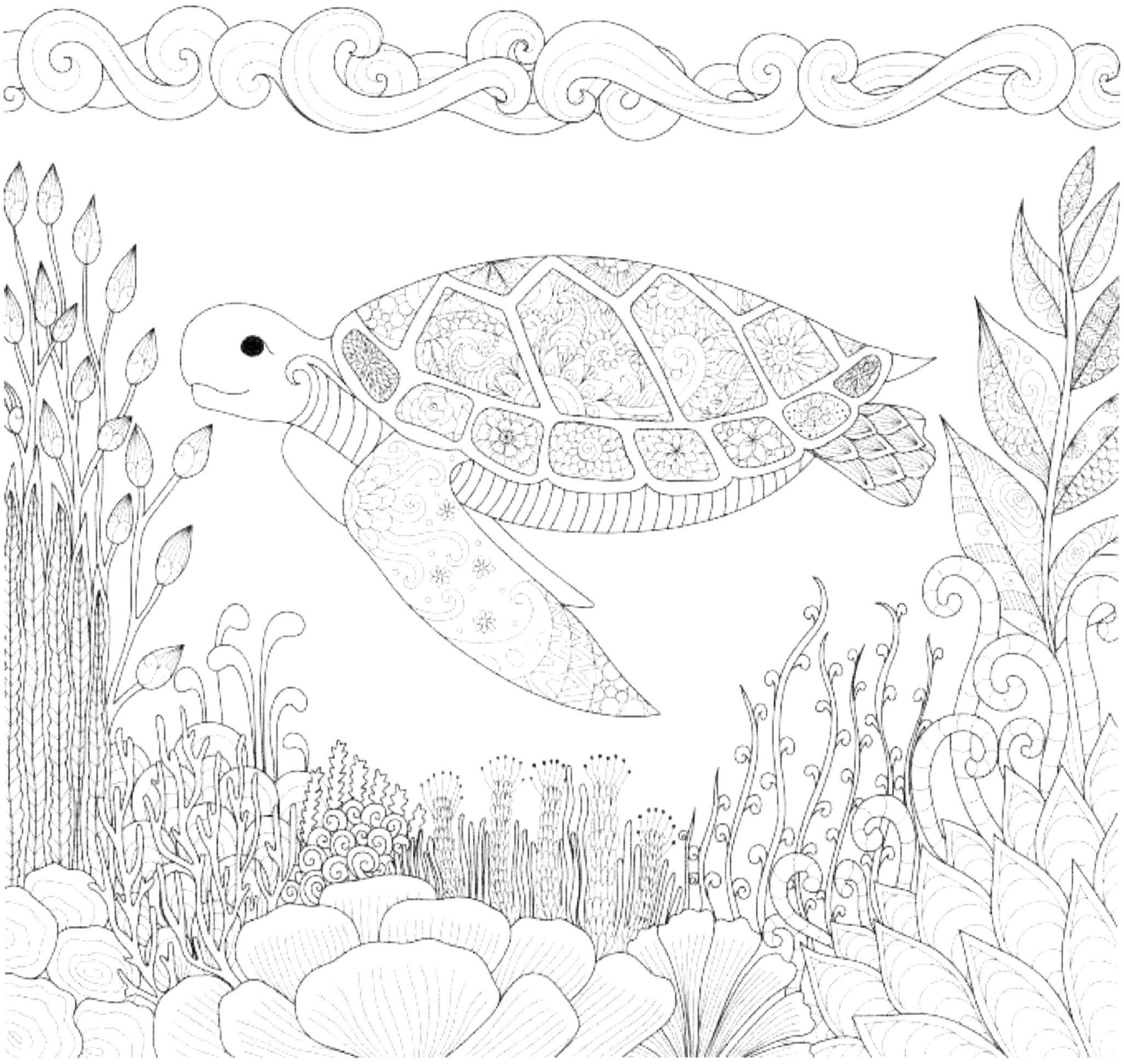

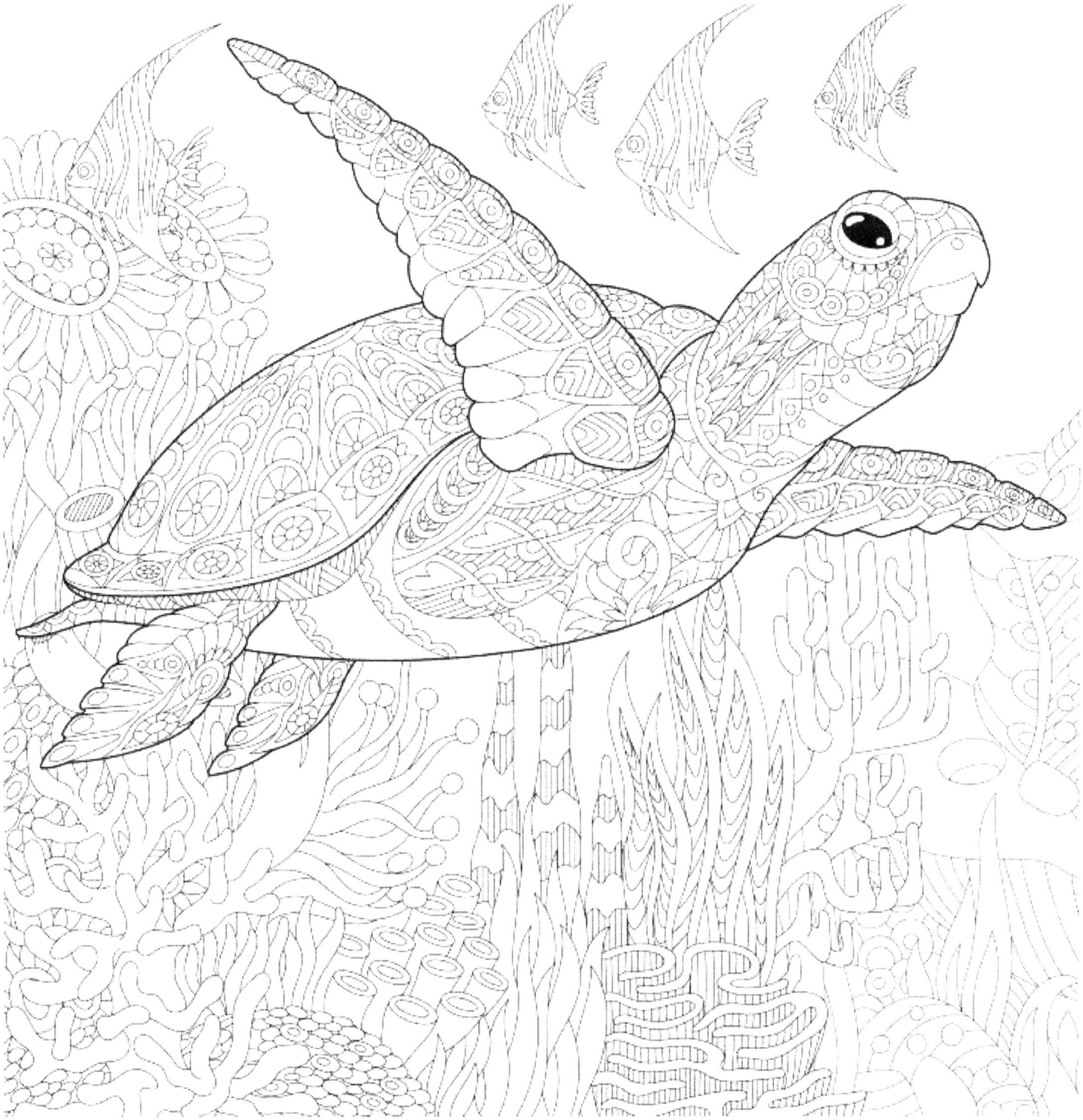

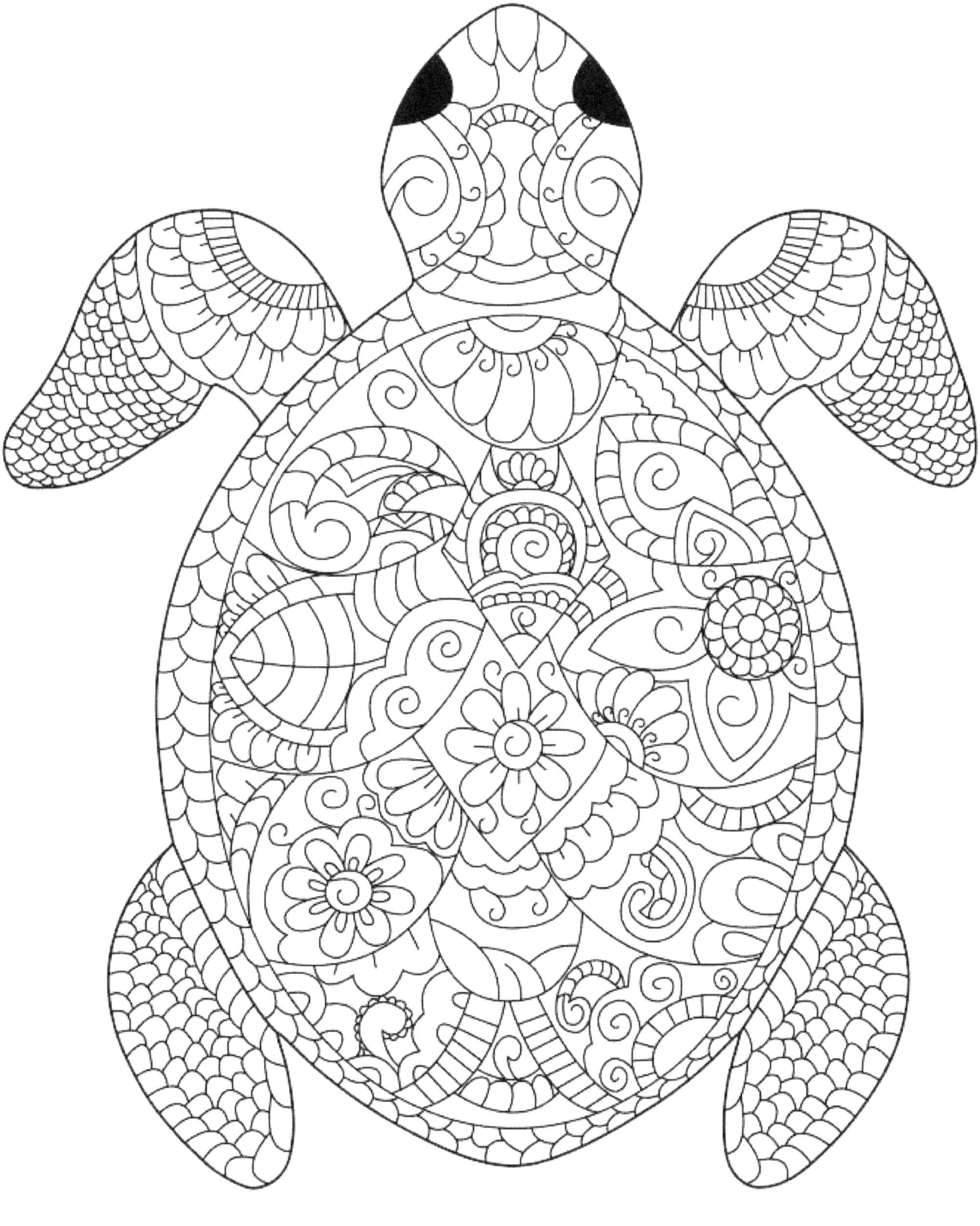

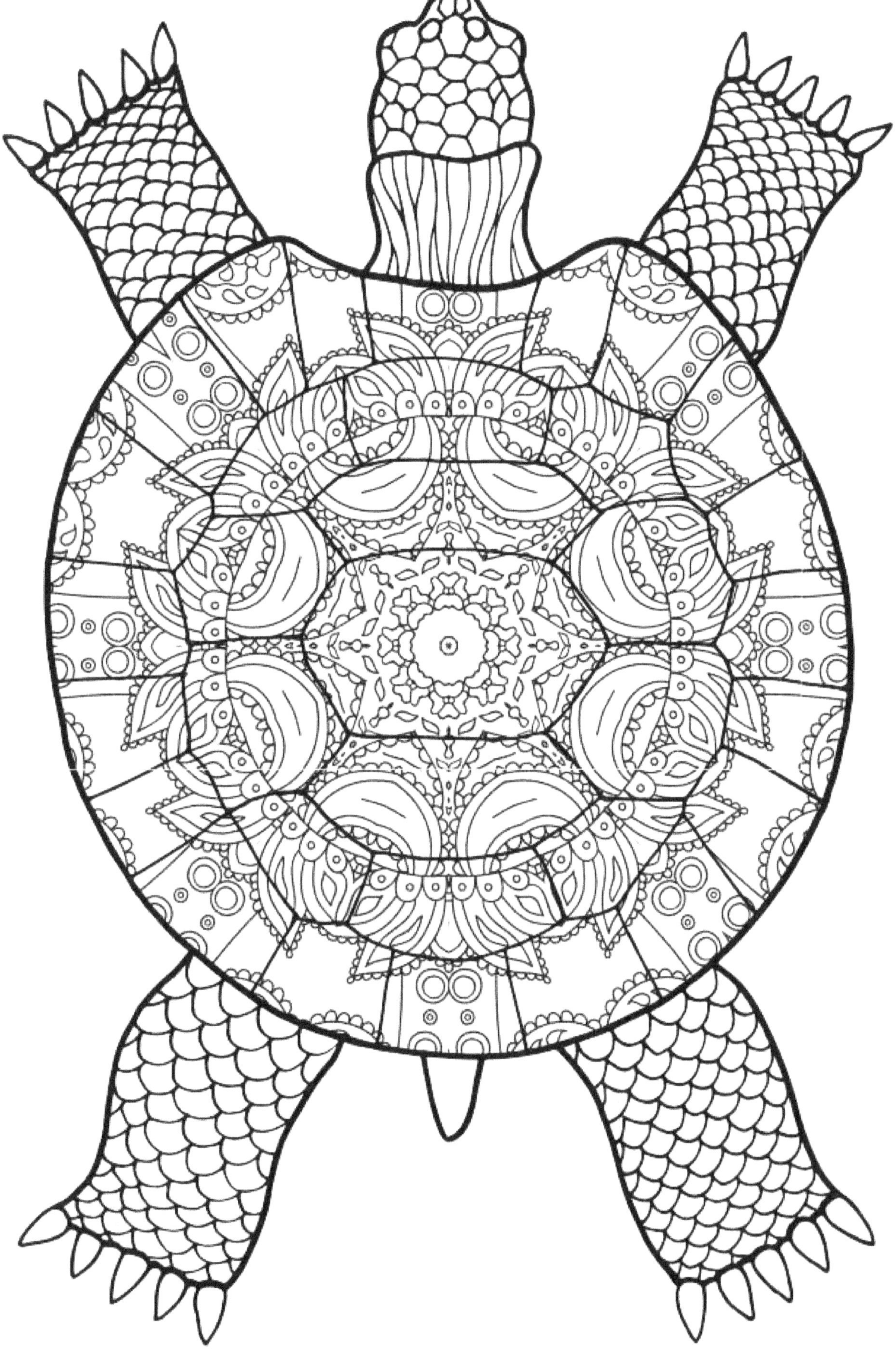

www.ingramcontent.com/pod-product-compliance
Lightning Source LLC
Chambersburg PA
CBHW081127180526
45170CB00008B/3034